Forms and Hollows

Forms and Hollows

Poems by Heather Dubrow

Cherry Grove Collections

For Timothy
With great respect for
your poetry and best
wishes,
Heather

Published by Cherry Grove Collections
P.O. Box 541106
Cincinnati, OH 45254-1106

ISBN: 9781936370221
LCCN: 2010942689

Poetry Editor: Kevin Walzer
Business Editor: Lori Jareo

Visit us on the web at www.cherry-grove.com

Acknowledgments

I am grateful to the editors of the journals where versions of the following poems appeared:

Artisan: "Instructions for a Student Essay"; *basalt:* "The Quotidian"; *Thebutchershop:* "One Morning That February," "Shades of White"; *Blue Moon Review:* "Accessory to some murders"; *Four Corners:* "Aged Cheddar," "Left Out, A Paradelle"; *Grist:* "Weather Report"; *HA!:* "Homemade Bread: A Baker's Dozen"*; Harvard Magazine:* "Our Lady of Murano"; *Graven Images:* "Waking Hours"; *Hampden-Sydney Poetry Review:* "Art Deco"; *Hazmat Review:* "Sydney"; *Hooked:* "Sage"; *Hurãkan:* "Lost in the Mail, Halfway"; *Journal of the American Medical Association:* "Flight Plans"; *Poem:* "Cordelia," "Twenty-seventh Anniversary"; *Poetry International:* "Garden Party," "Ring Cycle (I): Engagement Ring"; *Poetry Porch:* "Regret: A User's Guide," "San Diego," "Divorce Court (II)"; *Poetry Salzburg Review:* "Newlyweds," "Rue Daguerre"; *Prairie Schooner:* "Border Crossings"; *Sonnetto Poesia:* "The Baur Collection"; *Southern Review:* "Ghazal, Ghost-written," "Chance"; *Sou'wester:* "Rosemary and Rue"; *Southwest Review:* "Dill"; *Timber Creek Review/Words of Wisdom:* "Home is Where"; *Upstart Crow:* "Hippolyta's Wedding Announcement"; *Wisconsin Poets Calendar, 2004:* "Mourning in November"; *Wisconsin Poets Calendar, 2010:* "Autumn Sky"

Poems in collections:
A Tribute to Mairi MacInnes, ed. Peter Robinson (Shoestring Press, 2005): "Intervention"
Encore, ed. Elisabeth R. Owens (Parallel Press, 2006): "Moving Day"

Several of the poems in this book appeared in my chapbooks *Transformation and Repetition* (Main-Travelled Roads/Sandhills Press, 1997) and *Border Crossings* (Parallel Press, 2001). Special thanks to Mark Sanders and Ken Frazier.

I am very grateful to my research assistant, Anna Beskin, who efficiently and cheerfully assisted in the preparation of the manuscript, and I thank Amanda Calderón for her aid in proofreading it. Stephen Burt, John Hildebidle, and Angela Alaimo O'Donnell offered valuable help during its gestation period. The creative writing faculties at Fordham University and the University of Wisconsin-Madison warmly welcomed me onto their teams and taught me a great deal through precept and example; in particular, Ron Wallace brings exemplary acuity, warmth, and skill to both collegiality and poetry. Donald Rowe is directly or indirectly responsible for many of the joyous poems in this collection—and directly responsible for much of the joy in its author's life.

To my Fordham colleagues and students

Contents

I. Biopsies
Border Crossings.....1
A Litany for the Losing.....3
In the Hospital Corridor.....4
Shades of White.....5
One Morning That February.....6
Losses.....8
Mourning in November.....10
Waking Hours.....11

II. Precincts/Prospects
The Baur Collection.....15
Canzone from Manhattan.....16
Our Lady of Murano.....18
Sydney.....19
Intervention.....20
Autumn Sky.....21
The View from Chamonix.....22
Home is where.....23
Moving Day.....24
San Diego.....25
Rue Daguerre, Paris.....26

III. Herbs/Flours
Garden Party.....29
Aged cheddar.....30
Sage.....31
Dill.....32
Homemade Bread: A Baker's Dozen.....33
Weather Report.....35

IV. Venoms/Balms
Grey Matter.....39
motherlove.....40
Ghazal, A Map of Mirages.....42
Found Poetry.....43
Lost and Found Poetry.....44
Farmers' Market.....45
A Certain Age.....46
Chance.....47
The Return of the Native.....48
Instructions for a Student Essay.....49
Insomnia (III).....50

Revenant....51
Accident (I)....52
Cordelia....53
Hippolyta's Wedding Announcement....54
Flight Plans....55
The Quotidian....57
Art Deco....58
Family Christmas....59
A Walk on the Wild Side....60
You can't judge a book by its....61
Twenty-seventh Anniversary....63
Regret: A User's Guide....64
West of the Metropolitan Museum....65

V. Divorce Papers
Ring Cycle (I): Engagement Ring....69
Newlyweds....70
Resentment....71
Left Out....72
Jaggers and Jaggers, Inc....73
Divorce Court (II)....74
Rosemary and Rue....75
Lost in the Mail, Halfway....76
Aubade, for our Late Afternoon....77
We interrupt this program to bring you....78
Accessory to some murders....79
Ghazal, Ghost-written....80

I. Biopsies

i.

Border Crossings

To the memory of my mother, Helen Dubrow

In the hospital waiting room
during the November of my mother's life
I climb between the warm covers of my art book
and pull its glowing jacket over my eyes.
At the heart of its Mughal painting
a horse dies horribly—
lavender as its carousel changelings
but stiff as January soil—
under a tree as absurdly lacy
as cotton candy at an August fair
or mold
or the gauze bandage from her latest operation.
The painting, it will be obvious by now,
gives mixed signals, like my mother's disease.

Yet Islamic paintings recall those sets of Russian dolls,
nestling painting within border,
border within another border.
My dying horse is set off
by a yellow square in turn set off
by a blue square in turn—
well, you get the point.
There are three slender borders altogether,
embraced by the fourth, a spacious garden full of flowers,
where a halo of gold
giftwraps each blossom
in its own glowing singing margin:
Theirs is the perfect pitch of dawn in spring.

Ding potters, though I always knew them mainly
for their confections garbed in bridal white,
also caress and curve their winter darkness
into black bowls slim as April mornings,
which hold night firm within their fragile rims.
As for Louise Nevelson, I'm not certain
if she knew the violence of dying pastel stallions,
but she knew grief well enough
to joy in boxing blackness into pattern.

Meanwhile my mother lives a different blackness,
for past the margins where it all began

those cells grow luxuriant and uncontained,
her body a tropical garden
blooming death.

Meanwhile too my fear spills from its cover,
an ink blot falling soiling spoiling—on my art book.
And I wonder if the cancer drifts
from her genes into mine,
languorous and inescapable
as dandelion seeds on a summer breeze.

Even if I festoon my poems
with rhyme as sentinel at the ends
where the line drops into blackness,
all songs end on edges.
Even if I string my poems
with Christmas bulbs of cheery iambs
sooner or later the tree dries into silence
and becomes a fire hazard.
Sooner or later its fragrant cones

metastasize
as she edges ever closer to the border
of the cliff I cannot fence.

ii

A Litany for the Losing

Those were her results:
        the mended family quarrel and cushion.
Those were her results:
        the soufflés that sometimes rose, the laughter that always did.
Those were her results:
        silver that shined but never preened.
These are her results:
        the CAT scan she aced that first time.
These are her results:
        a trip to Spain squeezed in before the one to the operating room.
These are her results:
        thank-you notes finally written for all those damned handkerchiefs.
These are its results:
        the scalp that shines through.
These are its results:
        the news that can't be cushioned.
These are its results:
        sewing up without mending.

In the Hospital Corridor

Sikh turbans proclaim membership
in a clan of proud warriors.
Hers admits conscription
into another clan.

Her relatives never forget to come to the hospital,
& neither can she.
Her friends never forget to bring
comfort food from the most popular take-out menus:

CHOOSE ONE FROM COLUMN A AND ONE FROM COLUMN B:

my aunt's cousin had the same thing and says
it will grow back
I read all about it on the internet

in a few months
new medications are much better
it just takes time

Before, her house would have passed inspection
from even her mother,
now, she doesn't notice
that the stains too spread
far beyond the primary site.
Before, she remembered
even second cousins' birthdays,
now, she begins to forget appointments—

Tues Jan. 12 9:30 surgeon / try to reschedule cleaning woman
Tues Jan. 12 3:15 lab to check blood
Thurs Jan 14 ~~cleaning woman~~ hospital for chemo
Friday Jan 15 8 physical therapist
Monday Jan 18 ~~internist~~/ see his assistant? reschedule?

—but it doesn't matter much since
her boss keeps her calendar.

iv

Shades of White

Most white reflects. But this intensifies
everything, so that the nurse's gruff
Later burns sore skin. And the reply
of the young, condescending aide is rough
polyester preening itself as silk.
Yet buds of kindness blossom peonies,
that round, that June. The kid who brings the milk
brings the right words too, and his smile can ease
wounds. But fear—
Gangs of what-ifs cast shadows on white walls:
Sure, that pain may be gas, but it's so near
where the tumor was. There's the doctor in the hall—
Nervous questions. Cheerful answers. Yet doubts still rise.
For our doctors wear crisply ironed white lies.

v

One Morning That February

At the Museum of Natural History through Friday, a terrarium of live butterflies. Visitors may walk within the terrarium. Photographs not permitted. Admission fee: $10 adults, $5 children.

The overwhelming improbability of getting her there
despite the regiment of medicines
standing in attention on the bedside table,
despite what lives beneath her dressing,
Mother, you thought no one
would take care of your silver
as well as you did,
but I'm polishing it every week, and
despite the efforts of dressing her.

And despite her fears of the rambunctious taxi,
not surprising for someone who
I've done my arthritis exercises,
the way you told me to,
every week since you died
is being driven away from me
at one hundred thirty miles an hour
by her implacable chauffeur.

Her dizziness as we waited on line,
her hesitation at my insistence
I've kept in touch with some of your friends, Mother.
I sent Naomi those good chocolates after her operation,
But no, I won't phone Annette,
I never knew why you couldn't see through
that she be moved to the head of the line
(a woman in her condition, after all,
a woman impregnated by death).
A few things I could fix.

Inside at last in a world
where time flickers and pauses
like all these butterflies
Hey, Mother, you drove me crazy
worrying at my appearance all those years,
but you were right about one thing,
I'm using Dove soap now
as they land on her,
skin as transparent as theirs,

and almost thin enough for them to lift—

The overwhelming probability of butterflies
adorning the dying.
Mother, listen, when I wear your ring
its butterflies of light
pirouette off me.

vi

Losses

She was my lady four years, Mrs. Stanford was, ever since she took sick.
Always looked like a real lady even after that last operation,
when she couldn't hardly walk.
I'm going to start to cry again.
I loved her
and we talked about everything
those nights she was too sick to sleep:
my daughter and that stuck up man
my Marilyn wants to marry—he doesn't want to go out places with me,
doesn't think I look classy enough, doesn't think I'm worth much.
Mrs. Stanford always trusted me to put on the dressings,
never wanted the others to touch her.
And she had one daughter too, just like me,
and told me all about when she was a baby.
Her daughter didn't even say thank you last time.
Never cared how hard I was working for her mother.
She told me she was ready to die, it was in God's hands
I shouldn't do CPR but I know how,
I was a real nurse back at home,
I have my certificate in my wallet, right here,
just couldn't take the test over here.
When that Dominican woman didn't know how to help her
in the middle of the night
I didn't mind at all coming over and doing it
even though she didn't pay me anything for the night,
didn't even give me taxi money.
My friend said she was taking advantage of me,
but she was so sick she couldn't think straight,
for all her money she could hardly move,
and she needed me that night.
I loved her, my Mrs. Stanford, and I took such good care of her
that she lived longer than all those doctors said she would.
And that special chocolate cake I make,
uses real whipped cream, not that junk from a spray can,
she said she loved it and ate it all
even when she was too sick to eat anything else.
She always said what a good cook I was,
she would have wanted to thank me now.
That three hundred dollars lying here in the drawer now—
I always got money from the bank for her,
she trusted me, never asked that Dominican woman to do it—
she told me I'd get paid extra for those extra hours.

And I worked a lot for her, filled in when the other woman
didn't know what to do.
She looks like an angel now, like a jewel for God Almighty.
I fixed her up so pretty after she passed
so she'd look nice when her daughter saw her,
just like she asked me to, my lady.
We were so close,
I always did what she asked me.
How would that daughter of hers know what was there,
and with all their money they should have thanked me at Christmas at least.
She should have paid me for that night,
never worked a day in her life,
these millionaires don't know what it's like for us.
I did extra hours after that third operation,
when she couldn't move, my poor lady.
I can't help myself crying this bad.
But it's the will of God, and she's at peace.
Doesn't need her money now, poor Mrs. Stanford.
That bracelet lying right next to the money,
diamonds I'm sure, no rhinestones for my Mrs. Stanford.
That daughter of hers wouldn't miss it,
probably never even knew she had it.
It must be worth a lot,
she looked like a real lady when she wore it.

vii

Mourning in November

A clutter of bird cries
In air deaf as concrete
When daylight is terminal.

Widows of fallen leaves
Flaunt orange lipstick,
Fooling no one.

Chattering into midnight,
I stockpile bromides:
Hard and shiny as acorns.

viii

Waking Hours

Last night I dreamed the undertakers had left you,
smaller and perfectly preserved,
wrapped and rolled in a closet
among the furled umbrellas
and the Elektrikbroom Wonder
you'd planned to repair
before that first operation on the inoperable.
You were as light to lift as hope,
and I laid you on the bed,
making sure your tiny head was safely on
the pillow you plumped each morning
as you grew thinner.
Let me care for you again.

Unfurl your smile again, Mother,
and protect my head
from the cloudbursts of flashback.
Then let me bury you again.

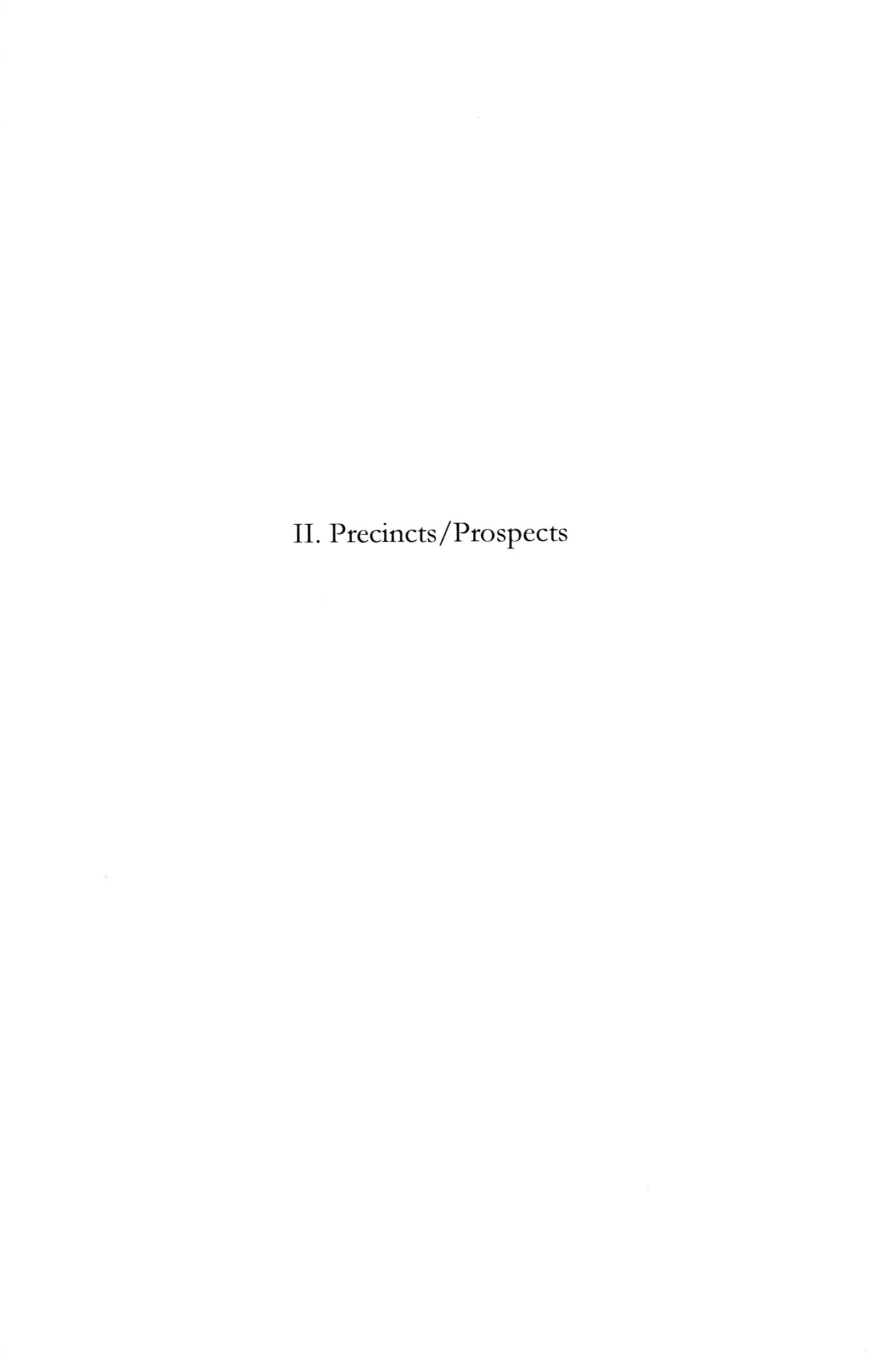

II. Precincts/Prospects

The Baur Collection

Admission: 5 Francs

Life, when it tries hard to imitate art,
Takes its cue from the sense of humor
Teenagers display. Thus witness Alfred
Baur, whose fortune from manure fertilized art,
Porcelain treasures.

Rose, a *famille* in which colors never
Quarrel. Pink buds perching like butterflies on
Creamy curves, and its peaches feeling
Furry. But also, there, Shino stoneware,
Sensibly greying.

Lacquer preens here in the dimness, shining
Subtly. Rivers like a lover's skin in
Moonlight: silver and as speckled. Pines with
Golden needles. And there water cascades:
Hair of a goddess.

Jade and nephrite in this corner lacing
Polyphony into patterns. Tendrils,
Shaped into baskets, here sing chords of grapes. There
Pale jade blooms into a lotus, humming
Vines over blossoms.

Swiss-born, Baur lived for some years in Asia,
Founding "A. Baur, the Ceylon Manure Works."
Eden once was there in Asia. He re-
Planted it with all its gardens intact
Here in Geneva.

Canzone from Manhattan
September 2003

From my Riverside Drive balcony
a picture postcard of a view
smiles for the camera,
sunning itself in the expected.
Now our three year old children are our principal terrorists,
and the bombshells we fear most
are the ones our kid brothers date.
And routine is a third grade teacher
warning us not to be late,
and grasping our hands to pull us away
from downtown.

> *"James James Morrison's mother*
> *Said to herself said she*
> *I can go down to the end of the town*
> *And be back in time for"*

The city gobbles the most upscale pastries,
and the most exotic teas.
Precipices are fenced with anthems.
The flags that made Park Avenue look
like a Boy Scout camp for investment bankers
are disappearing.
Curb your dogs
and fears.
We again believe in rhyme.
We sort and store away our memories.
We stockpile truisms, not canned goods or duct tape:
Lightning never strikes twice.
They'll try someplace else next time.

And yet
we still hold onto each other
like children crossing at a dangerous corner.
For curbs slope down

> downtown
> *London bridge is*
> downtown is falling down
> and is the Triboro Bridge really

Those who once insisted
on taking wine and witticisms dry,
now delight in a garage sale of clichés.
A twinge can seem like a dread prognostication
from a city declared in remission.

We walk our dogs and hopes as usual—
but doublelock all our doors
a little faster.
And as we walk we wonder
if that stinging at our heels
is a summer wind exuberant with soot
or the baby teeth of another disaster
biding its time.

Our Lady of Murano
Venice, 1993

The sexton admits us right before closing.
"One of the most influential instances
of fourteenth-century Byzantine art,"
I announce as we hurry in.
(Look carefully, she may be on the final.)
"Compare the Annunciation at the Victoria and Albert."
(I have eleven typed five-by-eight index cards on her
and a new PowerPoint presentation
instead of all those slides.)

A mother in a womb of bright gold tiles,
a bubble that will never burst.
She is slender as smoke,
or my faith.
Powerful as her own.
Look carefully, she is the final.

I try to recite to myself the four principal characteristics
of the Byzantine Palaeologue Revival (1260-1450),
the mantra of an unbeliever,
the tiles that pave my mind.
But cannot remember,
or only broken fragments,
as she rises above me
in a sky of unbroken gold.

This is no country for art historians.

Sydney

Ibises— looking for all the world
like some fantasy of monks
who poured all their passion for curves
into the margins of their manuscripts—
are alive and well in Sydney.
They strut through downtown streets,
as implacable and quotidian as pigeons,
and as improbable
as the greenness of the parrots
who live in the beige complacencies of the city's suburbs.

Some plants are familiar and well behaved:
old family recipes
brought over from England with the Spode china.
But the flame trees announce,
"We're not in Kansas, Toto"
with their bloodorange tongues.

And these buildings—
there, black lace that took a stiff drink
and danced the night away
(even New Orleans is jealous
of such wrought iron balconies).
Griffin built these Prairie School houses
after a stiff drink of Gaudí.
And here, Renzo Piano giftwraps brick
in shimmering glass.

No paradise to the convicts, of course,
or to the aborigines:
We taught them English, and their profit on it,
is they can talk to their social workers.
And entranced visitors
learn golden beaches have undertows.
This Eden, the guidebooks warn,
boasts funnel-web spiders and salt-water crocodiles
as well as kangaroos.
And the sun's a jolly salesman
peddling skin cancer to children.

But where else is a crescent moon
perfectly horizontal—
Australia's Cheshire cat.

Intervention

A pause in the recitativo
          of clouds
                    sings an aria
onto the lake:
Shining sterling against
          the industrial-strength steels
          of November.
Believe the sterling.
          Don't draw the curtains
          against its light
          to protect our furnishings.
Draw the light
against the canvas
of our doubtings.

Autumn Sky

In autumn the wings
of inkblack geese punctuate
the lucid blue page.

The View from Chamonix

i
Mont Blanc is

not nearly as full of itself
as one of those red roses.

contemptuous of the pyrotechnics
of madrigals and soufflés.

4307 meters higher
than anything cute.

courteous to Shelley,
but prefers reading Milton.

ii
Mont Blanc never

comes down with a headcold
or loses its temper.

listens to polyphony,
only Gregorian chants.

notices the tourists
or poses for their snapshots.

forgets an appointment
or a paradigm.

iii
Mont Blanc:
seldom predator
and never prey.

Home is where

every shoe in every closet fits,
though some are worn through
and most are out of fashion.

Home is where
the ghosts who rattle doors
at night in other houses
are cooking for us
whenever we come in
(pot roast and mashed potatoes,
lots of gravy)

and occupying the head of the table
wherever we try to eat.

Moving Day

Bodies get buried, their homes get tossed
Into cartons marked Thrift Shop # 3.
"The seller bears most of the closing cost."

Is your moving van big enough for a ghost?
Do your packers charge extra for memory?
Bodies get buried, their homes get tossed.

A seller's market, but death can accost
The most neon of brokers and set its own fee.
"The seller bears most of the closing cost."

The floors you can sweep, the fridge defrost.
But corners stay sticky with what I can't see.
Bodies get buried, their homes get tossed.

This bridge cracks and sways when it's crossed.
Burn it? Yes, but the flames singe me:
"The seller bears most of the closing cost."

Checks checked, forms signed, lawyers paid, Edens lost.
But this door can't be locked with any key.
Bodies get buried, their homes get tossed—
Catch, seller, and bear the closing cost.

San Diego

Italian cypresses insistently mark the graves
of half-remembered great-aunts
whose morals were as implacable
as their pasta sauces.
And Van Gogh cypresses are the lightning
intoned by Jove the Avenger.
But these California cypresses are wind chimes
rustled by some boyish god.

If all those sepia New England theologians
had visited San Diego,
they would have caught the error in translation:
surely Eve offered Adam a kumquat,
and even God couldn't resist a bite.

The would-be predators in this zoo
snack on Purina's Bird of Prey pellets,
and love their tasty neighbors
as themselves.
(Vulture chow? Only in California.)
One can almost forget the carnivores' cousins,
the slick species drunk on high octane,
revved up to inherit this earth.

Rue Daguerre, Paris
7:30 AM

I

Clichés glisten as determinedly as the croissants:
the boy who breaks and chews the end
of his baguette or craquant,
the cheese dealer who mocks
the fussy imperatives
of Common Markets rules and laws.
Memories of student days in Paris
nibble at the morning too.
But the coffee is strong enough,
the Art Nouveau carving melodious enough,
to turn
aura to aroma
pretense to yes.

II

This is of course the sort of neighborhood
where young men want to become bakers or philosophers
when they grow up.
There in the banlieux they smolder and burn
rather than baking and rising.

III

And even here the dog droppings
bud and blossom underfoot,
reminding us after all
that romance
is read and written
by those who wink
or glide with eyes half shut.
But if we navigate among
the detritus of dogs and ironies,
eyes neither wider nor more lidded than they should be,
Paris awakens us
to choruses
sung by flowerpots on balconies
and arias
by that alpha male of wine,
the Burgundy.

III. Herbs/Flours

Garden Party

Zwartkop aeonium:
a daisy with attitude.
As determined as a couplet
(& it wouldn't know from off rhyme).

These plants never get lost, even late on foggy nights.

Like other bullies
it wears its improbable Halloween costume
all year long.

No one can believe this flower
was ever a virgin.
These bad girls scare to death
the debutantes coming out at the Chelsea flower show.
These bad girls scare off
even gravel-voiced chain-smoking cactuses
in singles bars.

A flower that plays the tenor sax
in jazz combos.

Petals darker and more insistent
than a Rhone wine.
Stalks even a New York cop
would rather not mess with.

Aged cheddar

i

is the offspring
of a walnut and a Rhone wine.

ii

in its Francophile undergraduate days
wanted to be a Camembert,
but soon thought better of it
(trade the insistence of sunset
for the color of rice pudding?
give me a break).

iii

sends charitable contributions at Christmas
to those other cheddars
but doesn't give them its phone number or email address.

iv

chooses its crackers
with care.

Sage

I

You'd think this plant
couldn't care less about flowering.
True to its name, it goes in for an eminently serious green—
disapproving of the blarney
of emerald, that incorrigible flirt.
Knowing that limes
belong only in ice creams
(if there).
As for the opinions of sage,
they are measured:
It writes legal briefs, not madrigals,
as anyone who adds it to a stew realizes.
And it is well informed
about counterindications and side effects.
It views the energy of daffodils
the way mature cats regard kittens.
Dill pretends to eternal youth.
Sage knows better:
Its funeral plot is prepaid.
It sees through
the exuberance of mint,
that fast talker who never lets another plant
get a root in edgewise.

II

Yet from this indubitably responsible citizen,
which you would trust to write an airtight will
(let alone remember the shopping list),
spring flowers as delicate
as the song of a flute.

Dill

As rash and improbable
as soprano,
new dill in late October
trills upward,
Tickling as it brushes
its arthritic father.
Its tendrils write hope:
Maybe lost socks and chances can reappear,
and maybe even letters to the dead arrive.

Its next-door neighbor, middle-aged basil,
will have none of this sort of thing,
grumping towards winter,
wrinkled as last week's sheets.

But my dill insists:
Even that father
blooms shooting stars.
The autumn sun can rewrite
scars into
songs,
marches into
dances,
losses into
greens.

And green trumps brown.

Homemade Bread: A Baker's Dozen

I

The fragrance of perfume simpers.
The odor of bread smiles.

II

Bread rises
to the occasion,
like well baked thank-you speeches
at retirement parties.

III

Croissants pirouette into their basket.
Bread strides onto its board.

IV

The crust of homemade bread
has tolerable posture.
But for sure it's no West Pointer.

V

The color of wholewheat dough
is as laid-back
as a sleeping cat.

VI

And on the sixth day God saw
bread deserved no less a mate
and brought forth unsalted Danish butter.

VII

Bread goes well with stew,
and both are team players:
Hardworking, and they never miss a meeting.

VIII

Oven a little off? Sliced unevenly?
Bread forgives,
like other old friends.

IX

Cake crumbs maintain weekly
appointments with their manicurist.
Bread crumbs wouldn't bother.

X

Bread machines save time.
So does studying *King Lear*
from plot summaries.

XI

In the 60s I was an acolyte
of whole wheat, stone ground,
forgetting some pretty neat grandmas
croon white loaves.

XII

Suns pop out of bed—
like teenagers.
Loaves rise slowly. Confident.

XIII

The joy of kneaded bread:
Only one part of a man's body
is so elastic,
so smooth,
so happy to be touched.

Weather Report

For Cathy Yandell and Mark McNeil

I

Look: the lake is stiffening into silence.
Ducks in battle formation
assert their claim
to territory already half lost.
The sunrise is a damned liar.
Skid marks in the highway's snow
and that ambulance
warn that a phone call
can freeze fragrant mulled wine.

II

The hosts' rosemary plant says to hell with all that.
Its spikes survive against the odds,
determined
as a Puritan hymn.
Its green is so candid
roses feel ashamed.

III

Come— decorate this Thanksgiving dinner
with springing branches of rosemary.
Lift a glass to the relatives who would have been here
had their heartbeats not skidded.
The second toast: to those still here to enjoy
friendship as immune to frostbite
as our rosemary plant.

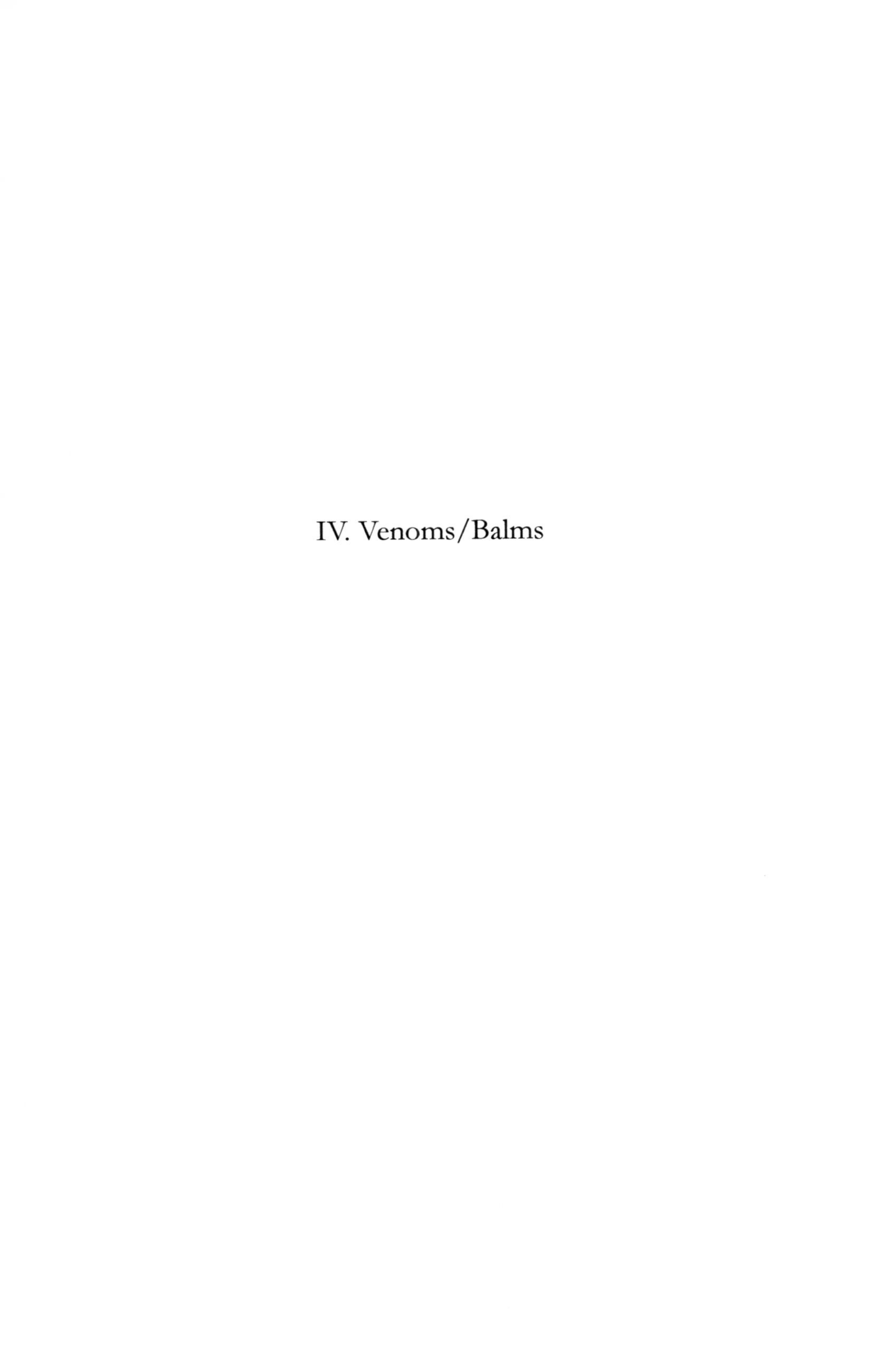

IV. Venoms/Balms

Grey Matter

i

These dreams are the curls of lyric
pigeons that sing Christmas carols
apricots who go ice skating
the roundness of bedtime stories
every green as frank as grass
No fruits moldy, no laugh bruised:
These dreams are the foam of morning.

ii

Auras are the brain gone naughty
lecture halls that smell of ether
light a symptom to report
coffee grounds or turpentine
doorbells hum familiar hymns
Pathology, not grace, writes visions:
Auras: orchestra without conductor.

iii

Memory is a noisy houseguest
garage sales run by grinning demons
rotting peach greens high school yearbooks
suitcases unpacked in stairwells
body piercing— birthday present
for its bound and breathless victims
No one leaves without a prize:
Memory is a naked twin.

iv

Fear is a determined mugger
words are rooms that spin to nausea
wind chimes with propeller blades
gifts of rags already lit,
smelling strong of turpentine
birthday parties turn to alleys
Ashes, ashes we'll all burn down:
Fear's the windmill of my mind.

motherlove

Listen to your dentist
(not only about flossing, although that's important too):

1) Cavities are caused by decay
2) Sensitivity to cold is a warning signal
of cold hands to come

Rosalind's heart ran away from home when she was twelve
because of the smiles and the doors
that were always locked

this is your new uncle Peter, dear
"I know a lot about little girls
all little girls like chocolate ice cream
you and your mother have such pretty curls
I'll buy you and your mother some nice ice cream"

say hello to uncle Michael, children

BUT WE'VE ALREADY HAD THREE NEW UNCLES SINCE DADDY DIED
(and this one smells like cigars)

maybe next weekend but you can't come home from college today because we're having a dinner party and

Rosalind's heart ran away from home more than once,
her future tied up in a handkerchief over her shoulder

until her eyes ran faster than her feet
so she untied the handkerchief
and as usual nobody was there to catch

maybe next weekend but you can't come home from college today because your special uncle and your brothers

Rosie, you have pretty eyes but
your mouth is much too large, not pretty

your mother has to tell you the truth

(fast forward thirty-eight years:

AM I A PRETTY GIRL, MOTHER?
well, Linda-sweetie, you're attractive but not pretty
your lips are the right size but your ears

some movies enjoy long runs)

The languages of those who see
behind and if only

never because or tomorrow
are hands unheld
iced words untranslated until they melt and make mascara run:

Question: Aunt Flora is dead? What did she leave me? She didn't leave me anything?
Response: But of course she left her children everything
Translation: All my cavities are very sensitive to cold now.
I married a nice dentist, he's a catch they said,
But he never took time to fill them.

Question: Did my new hairdresser do a good job or shall I go back to
Response: Don't worry about the money, dear, I'll pay for whatever
hairdresser you want to
Translation: do you love my hair   do you love   do you

(do you, Rosalind, take this
I do)

He gave her a new stone for every anniversary

We laid her in the cavity they had dug for her
with the headstone she requested— "Beloved wife and mother"—
paid for by the children who
could not read what it unsaid.

Ghazal, A Map of Mirages

Waiter, tell the chef I want my tomatoes but not my skin sundried.
Aging is a surprising salad. Hopes, test results, wit sprinkled on top, all dry.

Since you left, faucets only gasp and choke.
Sunrises could care less. Even carrot cake is dry.

Now our wedding album and our family jokes have stains
like rust. Acid seeping, plush covers cracking, drying.

The basement. My eyes and towels are still damp. Imbalance Warning on
my machine. And other tenants using all five of the dryers.

I'm gonna wash that man right out of my hair: the truth dawned
on me. Memories in mothballs, kid. But *if-only's* won't dry.

My philodendron played tennis at seventy-eight. Yet it just died
suddenly. While zinnias and heathers turn to straw. But we were always dry.

Found Poetry

SOLDIERS INVADE PASTORAL PARADISE
EYEWITNESS REPORTS OF MURDERS DISCOVERED
34 SHEPHERDS MISSING, FEARED DEAD
London Times, September 12, 1596

Cor don anishes ie shepherds o
pas o al
he oic seein pasto all
his doesn't
invasion

he open endin shephe ds Coridon

a lo ss s ing

Lost and Found Poetry

WARNING   ERROR   WARNING

A fatal exception has occurred

qualifying your computer for hospice care & enhanced drug benefits.

Your machine has performed an illegal operation & will be

1)reported to the American Medical Association

2)beaten into submission

3)beaten into ploughshares

All data that has not been saved will be

lost

but saved by Jesus

praise the Lord!

Farmers' Market

What a great harvest this year!
Even we city kids sparkle and gleam
when we find the four-carat red peppers,
the baguettes of kernel on the perfect ears.
And Richard was harvested too early, this April.
Linda cropped so quickly her husband barely got home,
Helene, whose warmth turned sellers into givers.
What jewels for their new boxes.
And Naomi, who—

Wait, now Niki is prone,
and a line of visitors at her door,
bringing

gourmet chocolates, bittersweet,
smiling mouths, full of feet,
lies, scythes,
spiffy tote bags packed with hope,
IV needles full of dope,
handkerchiefs, nice warm mittens,
stationery with the cutest kittens,
truffles, other gourmet foods,
plants and potted platitudes.

So let's stop at the cafe in the market
before there's too much of a crowd.

"What would you—"
"The apple cinnamon croissant"
Hey, what's cholesterol, what's overeating,

<table>
<tr><td>why save</td><td>TODAY ONLY</td><td>room for lunch</td></tr>
<tr><td>when Eve's</td><td>NIKI'S GONE TOO NOW</td><td>apples are on sale today,</td></tr>
<tr><td>heaps, so cheap</td><td>FRESH-PICKED FRIENDS</td><td>she's really giving them away.</td></tr>
</table>

"Here's your croissant. Next please, who wants—"

A Certain Age

Guidebooks, like other storytellers, lie through their teeth:
The Jensen shop, with its abstract massing,
striking colouration,
and careful detail,
still looks good
(copyright © 1985).
But in '04 Georg Jensen,
once self-satisfied as a cube,
is dislodged by Roots, Inc.
Logos and polyesters blaring through the loudspeaker
give me your hand and be my babe
as teenagers who spend fortunes
at John the Baptist's hairdresser
push in behind me. *Wasn't this once Georg Jensen's?*
And the manager with her own
aggressively colored hairdo says,
Well maybe but like a real long time ago.

But it is the changes in that dearer
building our bodies
that play the songs we cannot help but hear.
We have reached the age when doctors think
"How young are you"
will charm us.
We call our friends to check on biopsies, not recipes.
And the knees tell it like it is.

Now we can afford to eat in restaurants
where mushrooms and nuts cross-dress as sushi,
but their witty exuberance is held in check
by a décor that has gone to all the right schools:
Beige and black purr in pedigreed unison
(they wouldn't know from the crimsons of our youth).

Family members flatten into family photos,
or fill our dreams with the insistent
silences of Byzantine madonnas.

Dying is the change of life we'll share with men,
and in the meantime the grinning reaper plays peek-a-boo.

Chance

I

is a drunken driver
careening through stoplights and
retirement savings
as it sings God bless America,
getting lost on the way
to your home
but always finding it in the end.

is as inscrutable
and flirtatious
as a snowflake
in a windy tunnel.

is an obscene caller
whose voice you half recognize,
who always hangs up just before
you can be sure.

is a god who commands
rituals—
salt over the shoulder
and just for good measure
try crossing your fingers—
then rewrites all commandments,
informing believers
he reserves the right
to change prices and regulations
without notice.

II

Let's face it.
The myth of the fates
is all wrong:
Chance can't sit still
long enough to spin anything—
it has the energy of a kid
at six AM on Christmas
or of a metastasizing cell.

The Return of the Native

The determinations of orthodonture
lose energy in middle age.
Teeth shrug and sidle towards
their original anarchic positions.

The past shouts its nasal imperatives:
The mother's stiffened fingers
freeze the child's hand into a fist
despite the loud exercises of psychotherapy.

The high school yearbook photograph,
once shackled at its corners in the album,
saunters into the house, unannounced, at Thanksgiving,
depositing its sullen suitcase.

Instructions for a Student Essay

Submit an essay of EIGHT (8) to TEN (10) pages,
typed and doublespaced, on one of the topics
listed below. This essay is due March

Distrust theses:
they taste as metallic and insistent as a Metroliner.
Yes, sure they'll roar into the station on time,
but they leave tendrils of ideas
crushed beneath them.

Instead walk respectfully, slowly,
through forests darkly velvet with unanswered questions,
and stroke, never grab, concepts grazing among the bluebells.

Remember apt becomes pat
with a slip of the pen

31 at 4PM. No extensions will be granted.

Insomnia (III)

OK, for once I'll be grateful
I woke at 4:46:
clock smirking its wide-eyed digits at me,
husband purring sleep beside me.

Things I will do before 7:
1)Sort jewelery box
2)Discard divorced socks
3)Begin taxes
4)Send FAXes
5)Affix photos in book
6)Attach plant hook
7)Begin

But rain insists,
memories siren the dark,
yesterday stains all lists.
And photos slide out of their albums
and stalk up the steps,
as tight with fury as a Van Gogh cypress.

Revenant

We write because we can never rewrite:
Words won't erase, what-ifs still inveigh.
For acid reflux, take Pepcid each night.

You turn your back, your umbrella takes flight.
So do socks. But memories find their way
Home, where we write but can't rewrite.

Tide removes stains and makes clothes white.
But wine and acid don't bleach away.
For acid reflux, take Pepcid each night.

Should we call what was said that day a slight?
Words slight as a rapier but long lived as clay.
We write because we can't rewrite.

I'll decorate my house with dawns to fight
The wrong that rises due west every day.
For acid reflux, take Pepcid each night.

My magic carpets of cliché alight.
But that drunk driver truth comes out to play.
We write because we can never rewrite.
For acid reflux, take Pepcid each night.

Accident (I)

As confident as a mailbox
I attached myself to the sidewalk
and waited for the light to change,
sipping the sunshine like orange juice
on a morning composed by Gabrieli.

Yellow car
                the corner
bones & mornings
                        shatter quickly
the sidewalk slaps
        my leg
dead teeth in the street
                        my chain of pearls
                        broken.
        Kleenex tissue and finger tissue
                crushed next to each other

"Is she all right?"
        "She's not all right."

Dentists wave their metal wands,
teeth spring from the soil where money is sown.
A cheering squad of therapists,
all named Suzie and Barbie,
ministers the good news of exercise plans.
But I left my trust in weather reports
in porcelain fragments
stuck deep in the street's tar.
You can never believe those weathermen:
tornados swallow even
beds sealed with hospital corners,
lightning strikes twice,
cracking with laughter.

Cordelia

Truth is the most arrogant
of the single malt Scotches:
burning, stinging, singing
as it dissolves buttered lies.

Hippolyta's Wedding Announcement

They were introduced by mutual friends at a battle.
She walked away from a myth dark as dried blood
and co-signed the mortgage application with Theseus
for a penthouse condo with the insistent geometries
of the right neighborhood.
She has no name he can pronounce
(Shakespeare got that wrong too),
but an oncologist, highly respected by his colleagues,
will reattach her severed breast,
and her daughters will be satin.
The words that were spoken by her back there
have been planted too deep
for the most determined of journalists.
So her story and her face
will be made up
before the paper goes to bed,
and her heart unstrung by them
like her bow.
The years before he entered will be erased
so that Act I can be performed.
He is the son of Poseidon and Aethra;
before retiring, his father was a sea god.
She is the daughter of many mothers,
none of whom can make it to the wedding.

Flight Plans

To the memory of Hilliard Dubrow, MD and Stephen Gumport, MD

One weekend in May. They built it together,
my father and Steve, colleagues and friends.
When I broke my arm, I denied I'd been running,
well, maybe a little—so Steve wrote in his records,
"Broken while trotting around her house."
My father greeted octogenarian widows,
ailing after hysterectomies,
"The good news: I'm sure we caught it in time.
Bad news: I insist—no sex for six weeks."
They operated together, my father and Steve,
but that day they operated with glue,
and the plane was quite a tricky case—
they cemented it with laughter and luck,
but patient compliance was very poor.
The room smelled of Duco and dark Belgian beer,
and I carried their drinks to them so proudly.
When I slipped on some plywood and shattered a bottle,
they hugged me and said I was tall for five
and the beer didn't matter at all.

Early morning in June. Air soft as a mint leaf.
The schoolyard is bare and sunny and silent,
waiting for them and their big wooden toy.
It roars and coughs, chokes and sneezes
(model planes and motorbikes always have colds).
Their laughter curls and blows like their hair,
and the wind is a tomcat batting their plane.
At first it shakes, then rises—then soars,
brave in the bare and sunny sky,
so high its wheezing can't be heard.
When it finally trembles, then crashes and shatters,
they pick up the pieces and soon they laugh.
Nothing that mattered much crashed back there.

It was summer, some forty years later.
Steve's fingers grew stiff from Lyme disease.
A few years later, his heart trembled and crashed.
Three years after, in June, my father's heart too.
The religious right would claim they are gone
to the pilot whose planes never fall,
but the sky is bare and sunny and silent,
and Camp Winiweg rents that schoolyard in summer.

Its Indian braves fly their team flags there
and shout victory songs in their color wars.
Yet sometimes in morning I put down my book,
hearing sounds like a radio out of tune,
and memories of their laughter will float
in the air over our schoolyard and then
no other sounds matter at all
as the past shakes me and shatters and soars yet again.

The Quotidian

I

Fear stalks the mind,
ancient and implacable
as those winged Assyrian beasts.
Desire bursts file cards
into orchids.
Fury makes a shoreline
that was into self-satisfied ripples
hemorrhage a tidal wave.

II

But it is the daily nuisances
that chap the mind raw
even in Julys.
Penelope, dry-eyed and tight-lipped
when she heard all those rumors about Calypso,
cries with vexation
when the thread on her loom gets tangled.
OK, I'll grant you, broken legs
are a lot worse for the health,
but the splinters of the quotidian
turn the silky days they penetrate
to the burlap of November.

III

Heroism sings tenor arias
to the clashing tymbals of death.
But a lot of good it'll do you
when the piano tuner doesn't show up on time.

Art Deco

Brassy is beautiful,
Deco insists.
These colors wouldn't know
From grass or from sunshine:
The hands of this palette
Always point to midnight.
Metals mate loudly
As the whispering tendrils
Hymned by Art Nouveau
Stand taller and straighter,
Tango into diagonals.

The platitudes of rainbows,
Furry and friendly,
Yield to imperious assurance.
Pastels smile nervously,
Then simper into transparency,
Under the pitiless gaze
Of Deco maroons.

These self-regarding gazelles
Keep puppies off the ark.
Deco—the diet of tough cookies,
The brandy of champions.

Family Christmas

At first, to be sure, the rituals of kinship ties
are sorbet in fine crystal proffered between courses,
cleansing old anger soured between our teeth—
family stories we recall, dead names like icons we caress.

But as the evening ages, its joints swell and redden.
Memories of old insults are as familiar to the touch
as the oak tree we all climbed. As cracked and hardened.
We carve imagined rejoinders like jade brooches.

A nasty story, Christmas-wrapped as something funny,
sours the complacently oaked Chardonnay.
The adults slice and divide and bite politely,
as they watch the children playing.

Brief intervals of forgetting and fond peace
waft from the kitchen, smelling sensible as bread.
But soon even the children's shouts bring relief,
drowning those clamors that can barely be heard.

Brandy glasses offer golden distortions of our faces,
and the eggnog is sprinkled with cinnamon and acid.
Soon more quarrels twist and freeze like arthritic fingers
as we sing carols and one uncle dozes placidly.

She sews disparagement right beneath his skin today,
with her perfect, tiny stitches.
She is known in the family for delicate embroidery,
and he for his perfect pitch.

He has fantasies of hurling the pink demitasse
cup brought her by her grandmother from France,
cradled between layers of underwear and its sachets,
at his smiling scented aunt.

And so our Easter dinner will also be as fragile
as those pastel painted eggs a cousin once made.
Anger will swell round and hard in April,
burgeoning like a magnolia bud or a diseased node.

A Walk on the Wild Side
The Louvre

All those years Chardin painted pitchers
with as much backbone as a Greek temple
and no less self-confident.
What gives them that glow
is the assurance of geometry:
the triangles that follow all the rules.
Like a good marriage,
these surfaces acknowledge depths,
but aren't dismayed by them.

Why then this beast of a painting—
hissing, retching, spitting,
reaching out from the upholstered complacencies of this wall,
reaching towards the polished containers of the other Chardins?
A side of meat like a wound.
A cat with bared teeth.
The pitcher trying to turn its back to all that,
praying to fall off the table
into another painting.
What was Chardin doing that far from home,
in that alley of the body,
just when he thought
the opening and closing hours
of the museum
were established and posted,
his career purring
in a catalogue raisonée?

You can't judge a book by its

cover, or a cliché like that by its limpness.
The heart of an artichoke
is blessedly free of those thorns
that signpost its ungroomed parameters.
But in Shakespeare's day "heart" and "art"
sounded alike.

Today's paper reports that a nurse
in one of the fertility clinics,
who always remembered that the root of patient
is *patior*, to suffer,
and always had time
for all the members of the health plan,
always returned their phone calls,
dismembered her husband,
allegedly.
Tell me about it.
J— wore polyester suits that, as one colleague said,
looked like they would burst into flame
if he went near a match.
J— always had two days' growth of beard
(not an easy feat).
He thought cheese came in an aerosol can
and told dirty jokes staring hard
at female colleagues in the hope they would
burst into flame too.
Yet J— collected silver salt cellars,
the French ones with glass linings
rosy as a Monet lily,
and the English ones with cobalt blue linings
as honest and determined as a Machaut mass.
But, speaking of honesty,
do the display cases with their faceted crystal doors
that held in all those salt cellars
also hold the truth about J—,
or were they just for show?

I— was as witty as fusion cooking,
as carefully packaged as a bridal gift
from one of the leading stores.
He was charming as the Prince Charming
who woke the sleeping beauty.
He beat his first wife,

mocked his second,
and cherished number three:
they lived happily ever after
all that
if #3 is telling the truth.
Which of these stories
covers the facts
and displays his heart?

Twenty-seventh Anniversary

We have been folded together so long
we fit narrow envelopes without creasing.
In making love we know how
to finish each other's sentences.
Our children drop by
when least expected but most wanted.
And the other children of the marriage,
memories of that bad autumn,
have stopped phoning in the middle of the night,
but still show up at holidays.

Regret: A User's Guide

Some memories scamper:
Walt Disney squirrels
with those adorable tails,
chomping on pastel pink acorns.
They wouldn't know from damaging
infrastructures or blueprints, and
everything they touch rhymes.

These rodents of mine
dine on the wires,
chew through dear neurons:
master builders of black holes
all over my roof.

West of the Metropolitan Museum

City spats splattering—hot markets, the bus
driver's loud insult— blister the thick skin
of August pavements. Tar boils. And a fuss
reddens, bubbles, bursts. The usual poison
pours from the sweating cop's lips. And then two
nasal ladies, purple with perfume, insist
that rude girl took their place in line—she, too
teary to protest, drops her shopping list.

And so I retreat to the ivory of museums:
Three scholars sit, cross-legged, calm as dusk, on a screen,
their lips are open: they sing together, it seems.
Pine needles and peonies, delicate lines clean
as flutes. Wait—are those blossoms or blisters? A crack
snakes from his lips. Needling words, poisoned black?

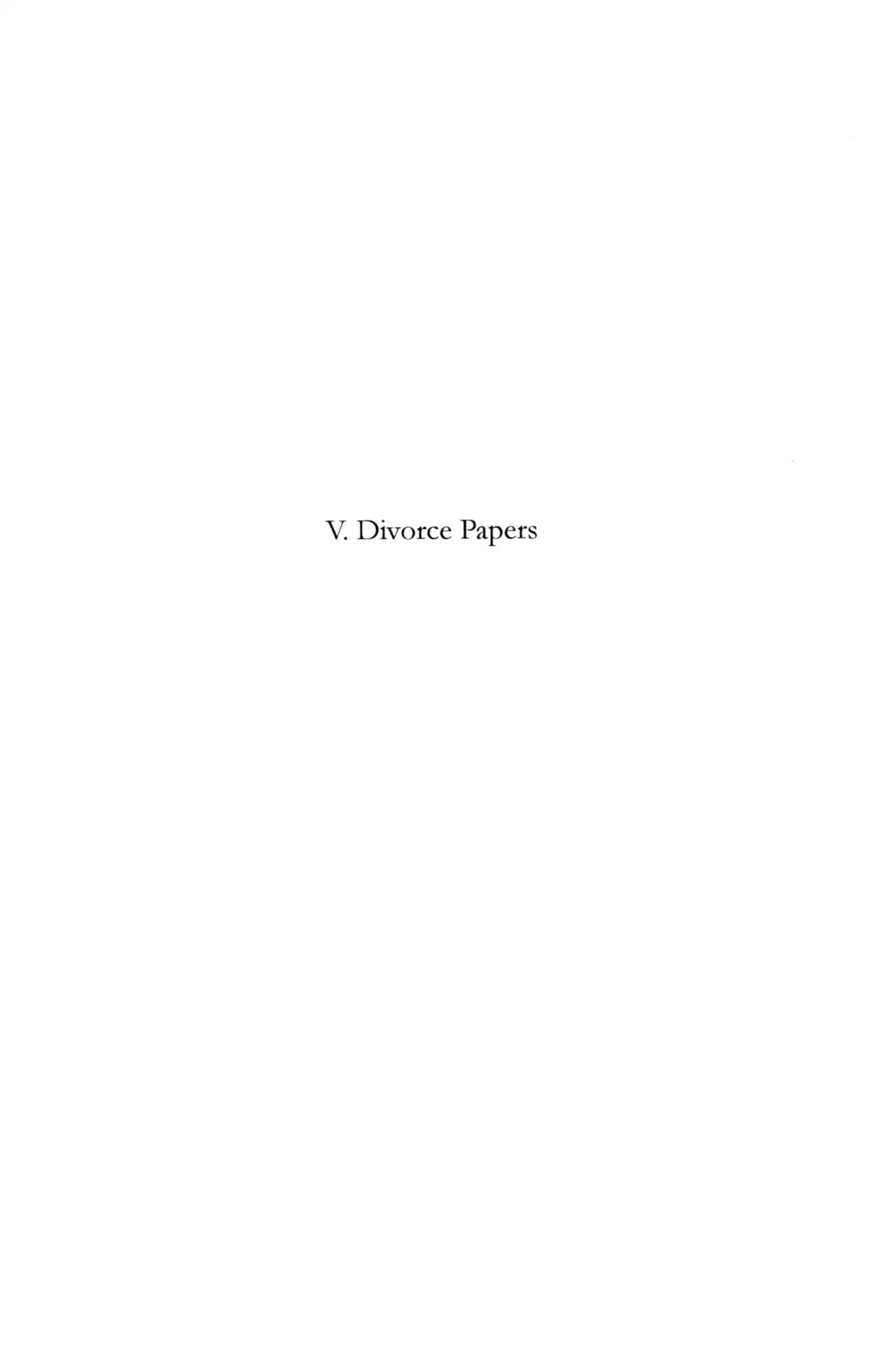

V. Divorce Papers

i

Ring Cycle (I): Engagement Ring

At twenty-three I thought that love chirped verse,
predictable as greeting cards. And my
new sterling forks and knives would fight the curse
of divorce: arms from the bridal registry.
'67: not diamond but sapphire
we chose, and a band braided like my hair.
A lovely stone, blue as the heart of fire,
and porcelain trying to look like stoneware.
Outside the jewelers, we see the proud
veterans. Protesters, chanting, block their way.
I wince and nearly cry because the crowd
threatens to trample my engagement day.
Not seeing the cracks in our brand new band,
not knowing the cold warrior grasping my hand.

ii
Newlyweds

The naïve exuberance
of a cherry clafouti,
authorized by Julia Child
(*Mastering the Art of French Cooking*,
Volume I, p. 655).
The placid reassurances
of towels whose borders
match the bedruffle and sheets:
a match made in heaven.
An enchantment of compliments,
madrigals sung to each other.
Each snowfall celebrated
with ritualistic snow walks,
covering us
with melting stars.

Not knowing the borders
surrounding this garden
would sprout blades of knives
as the first sign of spring.
Not knowing we returned
from all those snow walks
to our new carpets
covering black ice.

iii

Resentment

I

Years after I gave up on the toothfairy
I still believed our broken bottle
would doze into seaglass.
Spiked edges would mist and blur
into a whisper of that reddest hour,
hum themselves to sleep
and wake pastel.

II

When I was thrown out of Eden,
I won gardening classes as a door prize.
Lesson I:
Slivered glass planted beneath the skin
puffs into a ruddy blossom.
Lesson II:
A bulb of anger
metastasizes into a whole garden
of knives.
Final Examination:
"A dead marriage shrouded
in lawyers' linen paper
rises and prowls at midnight
among the blooming stones,
needing a quick drink."
Discuss.

iv

Left Out

A Paradelle

We are wearing this marriage casually, like comfortable shoes, and sharing lawyer jokes.
We are wearing this marriage casually, like comfortable shoes, and sharing lawyer jokes.
Old grudges untended, piled carelessly out in the rain, will soon be forgotten. Or wrinkle?
Old grudges untended, piled carelessly out in the rain, will soon be forgotten. Or wrinkle?
In this wrinkled, wearing marriage, we are sharing, carelessly and casually comfortable.
Will grudges be piled untended like old, forgotten shoes outside, and soon be in-jokes? Or lawyers reign?

When the marriage was new, we used to love our spring housecleanings.
When the marriage was new, we used to love our spring housecleanings.
But we thought what no longer fits could be hidden in the back part of the attic.
But we thought what no longer fits could be hidden in the back part of the attic.
We thought our spring cleanings could be part of love, too. But when we hid love,
Used, no longer new, back in the house's attic, what was the marriage no longer fit.

Anxious, we keep busy on the weekends, baking up thick brownies and polishing smiles for each other.
Anxious, we keep busy on the weekends, baking up thick brownies and polishing smiles for each other.
Suddenly bad memories, anger— as unexpected and insistent as a paper cut when reading, or like a burn.
Suddenly bad memories, anger— as unexpected and insistent as a paper cut when reading, or like a burn.
When anxious and suddenly angry, we keep busy, reading the polished smiles or the thick paper on weekends.
For we cut up each other, as insistent bad memories bake and burn like the brownies.

When our marriage was new, we thought untended cuts could be hidden or would soon be forgotten,
Like the old, wearied shoes, casually piled in the attic.
Weekends we baked brownies for each other, comfortably sharing unexpected jokes.
But as wrinkling memories suddenly spring back up, we are careless, anger burning out in the rain.
We keep busy cleaning the house, polishing insistent grudges, and anxiously reading lawyers' thick papers.

What no longer fits in: we used to love.

v

Jaggers and Jaggers, Inc.,
Specializing in Domestic Law for Eleven Years

Drive-through meals of divorce here. Served real quickly!
Take the special, the fast decree, and hold the
Blood. Yes, nowadays splitting can be painless.
Skip attorneys with Hermes ties and paper
Thick as linen, and go for lawyers who are
Cheaper. Elegance, no. Our clever partners
Neatly, rapidly pull asunder all that
God assumed had been tightly joined forever.

Turn at 7-11, straight away a
Sharp right. Clients have often turned all wrong and
Gone left into meadows blooming hopes once
More. If walking, beware, since every corner
Gets so slippery: second thoughts and maybes
Make it harder to dine on crisp conclusions.

vi

Divorce Court (II)

A whole toolbox of carpenters can't fix yesterday,
tomorrow shrugged and ran off with the family silver,
lost plots tap dance as they juggle
our arsenal of steak knives.

Yes, your honor, an irreparable breakdown
of that lovely wedding china
when I threw it
our bridal registry ensures that your marriage starts
an irreparable breakdown
of promises and platitudes
you two seem made for each other
and an irreparable breakdown
of my car which is why I was late to the hearing
and late to the seeing and knowing for that matter.
the wife is the last one to know.

The patient is a twenty-four year old Caucasian marriage
presenting with a general feeling of malaise and exhaustion.
Reports a family history of happy marriages.
Previous history includes suspicion
of unexplained late nights at the office.
On clinical examination a 2 cm. cyst
of anger discovered in the lungs,
metastasis to the heart
cannot be ruled out pending further tests.

vii

Rosemary and Rue

There's rosemary, that's for remembrance. Pray you, love, remember.... There's rue for you, and here's some for me.... O, you must wear your rue with a difference.

Hamlet

The married promulgate
family jokes.
They institute
state historical societies,
establish with spotlights
drawers of guest towels.

The divorced meet each other
in the hollows of monuments.
It was windy
and too dark for photos.
Yet even there, even then,
you taught me to plant bulbs.

viii

Lost in the Mail, Halfway

My old husband, my new postcard. Safely lightened,
as public as the sky, your voice is ballpoint script.
Your words sit demurely, their backs stiff, as though ironed
wrinkle-free onto this card, and a clean pale blue,
like a great aunt's birthday greetings, cheerful and prim.
One can iron and starch and fold our shards and ruins.

I remember our last meeting, and its ruin.
An April morning, my room full of sunlight,
thoughts folded, hands pleated on a straight-backed chair, prim.
My words packaged and wrapped, a proofread, indexed script.
But your eyes were not safe—as always sharp and blue.
And my voice parched, all smiles wrinkled, no longer ironed.

Now, two years into loss, my dreams still taste of iron.
I fertilize weeds, bordered with rue and ruin.
Still I remember a chance meeting—your eyes blue
as zinnias, and as I passed by they lightened,
much easier to read than this copperplate script.
Now memories too must be folded, starched and prim.

Back then our only script was runes of lightning.

ix

Aubade, for our Late Afternoon

For D.W.R.

I muse that new love at our age
is as improbable as a flowering cactus
when I wake with you
at dawn.

Your breath perks and snuffles as you stir,
like our old-fashioned coffee pot.
(Anyone but a lover would say you snore
at dawn.)

The valley between your shoulder blades
curves to cradle and warm my chin:
irrefutable argument from design. Till you flip over
at dawn.

Love is as familiar and unsettling
as the mischievous games of menopause
when I wake with you
at dawn.

x

We interrupt this program to bring you

I hear you died five minutes before a professional conference call, time enough to turn my briefcase into a shield, I sing arms and the academic warrior. Time enough to toughen into leather too. Memories—a handful of daisy petals, mostly something rancid far back on the lowest shelf—they try to interrupt the call. "Operator, this is a matter of life and death." Our committee agrees unanimously on the selection of two Honorary Fellows.

My father's unrealized wish to travel down the Nile leaves a cozy melancholy, burnished yellows and browns. But the years you should have had bleed to death, unread and unwritten books turn crimson, then dissolve. Alternative scenarios, those manic whores, flash their skirts to the music of phones ringing with undelivered lives from silent callers.

Psych 101 is my shepherd, I shall not want. It leadeth me to analyses shiny as the briefcase. It tells me this is bound to be really complicated. Explanations, rationalizations line up on the mantelpiece like so many tin soldiers. While other battles—pity squaring off against anger, unspoken words loading bullets surrendering loading again—knock down the toys. Surely goodness and mercy go out the window during a divorce like ours, and I shall dwell forever in this house of half-open doors above treacherous cellars.

xi

Accessory to some murders

After our green building cracked and exploded and the final decree filed in, back stiff as playing cards, I kept dreaming you had killed someone. The body was decomposed in lime, and you told me about it in the dream, handing me complicity, my hands clean, my fingers twisted into yours as you held me. *He killed a marriage*, a kindly friend glossed the dream, closing its windows, building me a shelter from guilt

Never really killed off by that explanation, the dream kept prowling at midnight, thirsty. Time for a housecleaning. Pictures, letters, executed with scissors through their hearts. What-ifs uprooted, bundled into garbage bags, with two Saftie-Ties. *May is the month when experienced gardeners prevent the plant from taking over their new garden. Pour poisonous words on it twice a month. Be sure to close the herbicide jar tightly if you have children. May be fatal* to whom. And so I composed poems, burying you in sonnets, tying you up into couplets. Meanwhile my jokes inflict paper cuts on you, *she's such a card,* some of my friends said, while the ones with sharper eyes and tongues kept their silence.

The dream goes into remission, lime is nothing more than part of a gin and tonic, and I sip recovery, composed, on airy balconies. I play cards and stories in trustworthy evenings. When that phone call breaks into my house. I never dream you killed someone now that you are dead, but I should have known earlier that dreamers who play with death had better hold all the cards.

xii

Ghazal, Ghost-written

One wishes ghosts were well bred enough to know they needed an invitation to return.
Queued like Englishmen at the bus stop, umbrellas folded, waiting their turn.

The date it happened, I remember it each year, I unfold memories packed in tissue.
I look out the window for you all day, but you come when my back is turned.

Away from yesterday. As determinedly perky as a hair bow. I gossip with old friends:
The arrogance of SUVs, dare we wear minis, White House interns.

One wishes he would behave like a sonnet, that is, the more conventional
Ones (forget Sidney), structured predictably, with the customary medial turn.

I have my act together, a scene of flowers arranged within an inch of its life.
Heathers and bromides blooming in crystal containers. Your turn. Your return.

Heather Dubrow, director of the Poets Out Loud reading series, is the John D. Boyd, SJ, Chair in the Poetic Imagination at Fordham University, where she wears two hats, the headgear of a literary critic and the beret of a poet. She has previously published two chapbooks, *Transformation and Repetition* (Sandhills Press/Main-Travelled Roads) and *Border Crossings* (Parallel Press), and her play "The Devil's Paintbrush" was produced by the Brooklyn Heights Players. Among the journals in which her poetry has appeared are *Journal of the American Medical Association, Prairie Schooner, Southern Review,* and *Southwest Review,* and one of her lyrics was the featured poem on the Poetry Daily web site; two of the poems in this collection, "Dill" and "Waking Hours," have been set to music and performed. Her work has also been reprinted in collections, such as *Encore* (Parallel Press). Wearing the other hat, she is the author of six books of literary criticism, most recently *The Challenges of Orpheus: Lyric Poetry and Early Modern England* (Johns Hopkins), and of numerous essays on literature and pedagogy; co-editor of a collection of essays; and editor of a forthcoming edition of *As You Like It.* Her previous academic affiliations include Carleton College and the University of Wisconsin-Madison; at Wisconsin she was the John Bascom Professor and Tighe-Evans Professor. Heather Dubrow and Donald Rowe live in New York City, where they delight in the poetries crafted by Deco buildings, Japanese lacquerwork, and French bistros.

CPSIA information can be obtained at www.ICGtesting.com
Printed in the USA
BVOW020534250112

281241BV00001B/34/P

9 781936 370221